Recipes by Catherine Quévremont

Tart Tatins

Photographs by Deirdre Rooney

sweet recipes

savory recipes

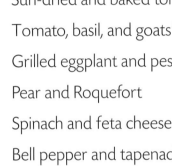

tips and tricks

First, a quick explanation of how the tart Tatin got its name. The Tatin sisters ran an inn at Lamotte-Beuvron in France. One day, the more absent-minded of the two sisters forgot to put the pie crust dough base for the apple pie in the bottom of the baking pan before adding the filling; having no alternative she simply put it on top.

If considered from a more technical point of view, however, the interesting aspect of this French equivalent of an "upside-down cake" is that the filling is cooked beneath a layer of crust, which prevents it from drying out in the oven. The pie crust lid retains a greater degree of humidity, and as a result the filling is almost steamed, which makes for interesting flavor combinations.

Which baking pan should I use?

A pan with a nonstick coating is best, because that way the tart will be easier to turn out, even if the filling has caramelized.

A fixed-based baking pan is essential to prevent the cooking juices from running out of the pan.

Before it is cooked, a tart Tatin is quite deep; the filling collapses slightly as it cooks.

For this reason, it is best to use a deep rather than a shallow baking pan.

Many different sorts of baking dish are suitable for making tart Tatins:

- Individual ramekin dishes
- A soufflé dish
- A square, round or oval ovenproof dish
- Even a cast-iron skillet: use it first to caramelize the fruit, then top with a precooked round of pie crust.

Tart crusts

A sweet plain pie crust is the traditional choice for making a fruit tart Tatin, but there is nothing to stop you using other types.

Puff pastry is better for fruits that produce a lot of water during cooking. Buy chilled or frozen ready-made puff pastry and follow maker's instructions for use.

Another alternative is to rub sweet pie crust dough with the fingertips until it resembles breadcrumbs, as for a crisp. Pat the mixture down firmly to make a solid crust base when you turn it out.

Alternative suggestions

- Cut a disk of sponge cake to fit the baking pan and place over an almond-and-fruit cream filling.
- Cut two buckwheat pancakes to fit the baking pan, then brush with butter so that they become crisp when cooked, and place over a fish or shellfish filling.

a selection of suitable crusts

Plain pie crust

1³/₄ cups all-purpose flour

pinch of salt

4 oz butter, softened

water

Sift the flour and salt together in a mixing bowl. Make a well in the center, add the butter and rub in with the fingertips until the mixture resembles large breadcrumbs.

Add a little water and knead to form a soft dough, adding more water if necessary. Leave to rest in the refrigerator for 1 hour before using.

Sweet plain pie crust

1³/₄ cups all-purpose flour

¹/₂ cup superfine sugar

pinch of salt

5 oz unsalted butter, very soft

1 egg, beaten

water

Sift the flour, sugar, and salt together in a mixing bowl. Make a well in the center and add the butter.

Rub in with the fingertips, working quickly so that the dough does not turn into breadcrumbs. Add the egg and a little water, and knead lightly to form a soft dough, adding more water if necessary. Leave to rest in the refrigerator for 1 hour before using.

Cornflake pie crust

4 cups cornflakes

5 oz unsalted butter

warm milk

¹/₂ envelope dried yeast

4 tablespoons cornstarch

1 tablespoon superfine sugar

Crush the cornflakes coarsely using a rolling pin, then transfer to a large mixing bowl.

Soften the butter in a microwave oven, then combine with the milk and yeast.

Add the cornstarch, sugar, milk, and melted butter to the crushed cornflakes and combine to produce a soft dough.

Parmesan pie crust

1¹/₂ cups all-purpose flour

1 teaspoon table salt

1 cup freshly grated Parmesan cheese

¹/₂ cup freshly grated Gruyère cheese

¹/₂ envelope dried yeast

2 eggs

1 teacup milk

2–3 tablespoons mustard

4 oz unsalted butter, melted

Sift the flour and salt together, add the Parmesan and Gruyère cheeses, and the yeast. Beat the eggs together with the milk and add to the flour mixture. Knead to form a smooth dough, then stir in the mustard, followed by the melted butter.

Apple Tatin

Serves 6

5 apples: Golden Russet,
Braeburn, or Cox's
Orange Pippin

4 oz butter

3 tablespoons sugar

½ teaspoon vanilla extract

8 oz plain pie crust dough
(see page 5)

Preheat the oven to 400°F.

Peel and core the apples and cut into ¾-inch thick slices.

Melt the butter in a skillet and fry the sliced apple for
1–2 minutes on each side until golden.

Sprinkle the sugar over the base of a baking pan, arrange
the apple slices evenly on top, and sprinkle with the vanilla
extract. Top with the rolled-out pie crust dough, making a
small hole in the center to allow the steam to escape.

Bake for 10 minutes, then reduce heat to 225°F and bake
for a further 20 minutes.

Remove from the oven and immediately turn the tart out
onto a serving dish. Serve with sour cream, whipped cream,
or a scoop of vanilla ice cream.

Apricot Tatin

Serves 6

12 firm fresh apricots

2 oz unsalted butter

1 tablespoon olive oil

2 egg yolks

4 tablespoons sugar

1/4 pint sour cream,
or creamy yogurt

1/4 cup pine nuts, toasted

8 oz ready-made puff pastry

Preheat the oven to 225°F.

Halve the apricots and remove the pits. Heat the butter and oil in a nonstick skillet and fry the apricot halves for 2 minutes on each side until golden. They should remain firm. Place on paper towels to drain.

Meanwhile, beat the egg yolks together with the sugar and sour cream.

Arrange the apricot halves in the base of a baking pan, cut sides up, sprinkle with the pine nuts and pour over the egg and sour cream mixture. Top with the rolled-out puff pastry, pressing down firmly to seal at the sides of the baking pan.

Bake for 10 minutes, then increase the heat to 350ºF and bake for a further 20 minutes.

Pear Tatin

Serves 6

4 tablespoons sugar

1 vanilla bean, split in half lengthwise

3 pears, Comice if possible

½ cup raisins

2 tablespoons rum

3 eggs

2 tablespoons ground almonds

8 oz plain pie crust dough (see page 5)

In a large pan, heat 1¾ pints water with the sugar and the vanilla bean until the sugar has melted. Peel and halve the pears, remove the core, place the pear halves in the sugar syrup and cook for 10 minutes. Remove the pears with a slotted spoon and leave to drain on a wire rack. Reserve the syrup.

Place the raisins in a bowl, sprinkle with 1 tablespoon of the rum and 2 tablespoons of the reserved pear syrup.

Preheat the oven to 350°F.

Beat the eggs together with the ground almonds and the remaining rum.

Arrange the pears, cut sides up, in the base of a baking pan, scatter over the raisins and cover with the almond mixture. Top with the rolled-out pie crust dough and bake for 25 minutes.

Rhubarb Tatin

Serves 6

1½ lb rhubarb

3 slices gingerbread

½ cup soft brown sugar

2 tablespoons Irish whiskey

8 oz plain pie crust dough
(see page 5)

Preheat the oven to 350°F.

Cut the rhubarb in ¾-inch chunks.

Crumble the gingerbread slices. Sprinkle the brown sugar over the base of a baking pan, then add the first layer of rhubarb and sprinkle with half the crumbled gingerbread and 1 tablespoon whiskey. Add a second layer of rhubarb, then scatter with the remaining gingerbread and whiskey.

Top with the rolled-out pie crust dough, tucking it down well inside the baking pan. Bake for 45 minutes.

Serve with stirred custard, or whipped cream, flavored with whiskey.

Orange Tatin

Serves 6

3 unwaxed, or well-scrubbed, oranges

1 cup corn syrup (or preferably British golden syrup)

8-oz tub mascarpone cheese

2 eggs

2 tablespoons Cointreau

8 oz ready-made puff pastry

Remove the rind of one of the oranges with a zester or sharp knife and blanch for 2 minutes in boiling water. Heat the corn syrup, add the blanched zest and caramelize for about 10 minutes. Remove the zest with a slotted spoon and drain, reserving 1 tablespoon of the caramelized syrup.

Preheat the oven to 400°F.

Remove the peel and pith from all the oranges. Using a sharp knife, cut the oranges into quarters. Cut between each segment, but stop before you get to the center. Place the orange quarters to drain on paper towels.

In a bowl, combine the mascarpone cheese with the eggs, caramelized syrup, orange zest, and Cointreau, stirring well.

Arrange the orange quarters over the base of a baking pan and pour over the mascarpone mixture. Top with the rolled-out puff pastry, sealing the pastry edges well by pinching them against the sides of the baking pan.

Bake for 10 minutes, then reduce heat to 325°F and bake for a further 20 minutes.

Peach Tatin

Serves 6

5 white peaches

8 oz redcurrants

2 oz unsalted butter

1/3 cup soft brown sugar

1/2 cup blanched almonds

**8 oz plain pie crust dough
(see page 5)**

Skin and halve the peaches, remove the pits, and leave to drain on a wire rack or paper towels.

Preheat the oven to 400°F.

Remove the stalks from the redcurrants. Melt the butter in a skillet and quickly fry the redcurrants over a high heat, stirring constantly with a wooden spoon, for 7–8 minutes. Using the back of the spoon, crush any berries that have not collapsed during cooking.

Pass the crushed redcurrants through a fine sieve. If the juice is too runny, return it to the skillet and boil vigorously until it thickens. It should coat the back of a spoon.

Sprinkle the brown sugar over the base of a baking pan, add the almonds, pour over the redcurrant juice and arrange the peach halves evenly.

Top with the rolled-out pie crust dough, taking care to seal it well to the sides of the baking pan. Bake for 25 minutes.

Mango Tatin

2 large (or 3 medium),
ripe mangoes

3 passion fruit

2 oz unsalted butter

⅓ cup soft brown sugar

2 tablespoons white rum

2 allspice berries

8 oz plain pie crust dough
(see page 5)

Peel the mangoes and cut into thick slices, reserving any juice that is produced.

Preheat the oven to 400°F.

Cut open the passion fruit and pass the flesh through a fine strainer to remove the seeds. Melt the butter and sugar in a large pan. Add the mango and passion fruit juices and the rum. Boil for 10 minutes until very thick.

Pour the caramelized juice into a baking pan, and arrange the mango slices on top. Crush the allspice berries and sprinkle over the mangoes. Top with the rolled-out pie crust dough, taking care to seal it firmly at the edges, and bake for 25 minutes.

Cherries in brandy Tatin

Serves 6

1 lb fresh black cherries

1 lb cherries in brandy

½ jar, (about 6 oz) cherry jam

8 oz plain pie crust dough (see page 5)

Remove the pits from the fresh cherries, reserving any juice. Also remove the pits from the cherries in brandy, reserving 3 tablespoons of the brandy.

Preheat the oven to 400°F.

Put all the cherries and the jam in a large pan, together with the juice collected from the fresh cherries and the reserved juice from the cherries in brandy, and boil vigorously to produce a thick compote.

Spread the cherry compote over the base of a baking pan. For even more flavor, scatter over a few whole cherries in brandy. Top with the rolled-out pie crust dough, taking care to seal it firmly at the edges, and bake for 25 minutes.

Prune Tatin

Serves 6

1 Earl Grey teabag

14 oz prunes, pitted

¼ pint Armagnac
(or Cognac)

2 tablespoons soft brown
sugar

2 large fresh black figs

8 oz ready-made puff
pastry

Put the teabag into a medium-sized heatproof bowl, pour over 1 cup boiling water and leave to infuse. Add the prunes to the tea, together with the Armagnac, or Cognac, and leave to soak overnight or for at least 6 hours.

Preheat the oven to 425°F.

Lift out the prunes with a slotted spoon and put in a large pan together with 4 tablespoons of the soaking juices. Add the sugar and boil gently, stirring, for 10 minutes or until the prunes have softened to form a compote.

Cut the figs into quarters, arrange over the base of a baking pan, cut side facing downward, and cover with the prune compote. Top with the rolled-out puff pastry, seal well at the sides of the baking pan, and bake for 25 minutes.

Quince Tatin

Serves 6

3 large quince

4 tablespoons lemon juice

3 oz salted butter

2 tablespoons chestnut honey, or other good flavored honey

a few pinches of cinnamon

8 oz plain pie crust dough (see page 5)

Peal the quince, cut into thick slices and sprinkle with the lemon juice to prevent them from discoloring.

Preheat the oven to 400°F.

Melt the butter and honey in a deep-sided skillet. Add the sliced quince and brown in the butter for 10 minutes, turning frequently. Remove the quince with a slotted spoon and then boil the cooking juices until they have reduced to form a caramel sauce.

Arrange the caramelized quince slices in the base of a baking pan, sprinkle with the cinnamon and pour over the caramel sauce.

Top with the rolled-out pie crust dough, seal well at the edges and bake for 25 minutes.

Banana and chocolate Tatin

Serves 6

4 bananas

4 tablespoons lemon juice

2 oz unsalted butter

4 tablespoons sugar

1 teaspoon vanilla extract

½ cup semisweet chocolate chips

8 oz plain pie crust dough (see page 5)

Preheat the oven to 350°F. Peel and slice the bananas, then sprinkle with the lemon juice to prevent them discoloring.

Melt the butter, sugar, and vanilla extract in a large skillet, then carefully fry the banana slices until golden, taking care that they do not disintegrate.

Arrange the chocolate chips evenly over the base of a baking pan, cover with two layers of sliced banana, then top with the rolled-out pie crust dough and bake for 25 minutes.

Delicious served with a scoop of chocolate ice cream.

Pineapple and kiwifruit Tatin

Serves 6

6 slices fresh pineapple

3 egg yolks

3 tablespoons grated coconut

4 tablespoons sugar

¾ cup sour cream, or creamy yogurt

8 oz plain pie crust dough (see page 5)

3 kiwifruit

Preheat the oven to 325°F.

Arrange the pineapple slices on a baking sheet and bake in the oven for 10 minutes until they have dried out slightly.

Beat the egg yolks together with the coconut, sugar, and sour cream.

Remove the pineapple slices from the oven and cut into quarters. Arrange the pineapple pieces over the base of a nonstick baking pan, cover with the batter and top with the rolled-out pie crust dough.

Bake for 25 minutes. When cooked, remove from the oven and leave to cool for 10 minutes before turning out.

Peel the kiwifruit, cut into very thin slices and arrange over the tart. It is best not to cook the kiwifruit.

Blueberry Tatin

Serves 6

4 tablespoons water

½ cup sugar

1 lb blueberries

2 leaves gelatin (see note)

8 oz plain pie crust dough
(see page 5)

Preheat the oven to 350°F.

Heat the water and sugar in a pan to form a light syrup.
Add the blueberries and simmer gently for 10 minutes.

Soften the gelatin leaves in cold water, then squeeze to expel
the water. Add the gelatin to the blueberries while they are still
cooking and stir well to dissolve.

Pour the blueberry mixture into a baking pan, top with the
rolled-out pie crust dough, and bake for 25 minutes.
Leave to cool for 10 minutes before turning out.

Note: If leaf gelatin is not readily available, use 1½ teaspoons
powdered gelatin, following the maker's instructions.

Tomato and sardine Tatin

Serves 6

12 fresh sardine fillets

2 lb tomatoes

2 tablespoons olive oil

sprig of rosemary

8 oz ready-made puff pastry

large knob of butter, melted

sea salt and freshly ground black pepper

Preheat the oven to its lowest setting.

Carefully wipe the sardine fillets and remove any remaining bones.

Halve the tomatoes and place them, cut side up, on a baking sheet. Drizzle with olive oil, season with salt and place a few rosemary leaves on each tomato. Bake for 20 minutes, then remove from the oven.

Increase the oven temperature to 400°F.

Arrange the sardine fillets evenly over the lightly oiled base of a baking pan, cover with the baked tomatoes and top with the rolled-out puff pastry. Brush the pastry with the melted butter and bake for 25 minutes.

Turn the tart out onto a serving dish, season with sea salt and freshly ground black pepper and drizzle with a little olive oil if necessary.

Tomato and mozzarella Tatin

Serves 6

2 x 14-oz cans peeled whole tomatoes

1 garlic clove, peeled

bunch of basil, washed

1 tablespoon olive oil

1 (about 4 oz) buffalo milk mozzarella cheese (*mozzarella di bufala*)

8 oz ready-made puff pastry

sea salt and freshly ground black pepper

few sprigs fresh oregano, to garnish

Drain, seed, and coarsely chop the tomatoes. Chop the peeled garlic and washed basil.

Preheat the oven to 400°F.

Heat the oil in a large skillet and fry the tomatoes sprinkled with the garlic and basil and seasoned with salt and pepper. Cook over a high heat until the mixture is almost dry.

Drain the mozzarella cheese, pat dry with paper towels and cut into thick slices.

Place the cheese slices over the base of a baking pan, pour over the tomato sauce and top with the rolled-out puff pastry. Bake for 25 minutes.

Turn out onto a serving dish and sprinkle with the oregano while still hot.

Sun-dried and baked tomato Tatin

Serves 6

1 lb fresh tomatoes

2 tablespoons olive oil

2 garlic cloves, peeled and crushed

8 oz sun-dried tomatoes in oil

1 teaspoon ground cumin

2 tablespoons olive oil

8 oz plain pie crust dough (see page 5)

sea salt and freshly ground black pepper

arugula leaves, to garnish

Preheat the oven to its lowest setting.

Cut the fresh tomatoes into $1/2$-inch thick slices and place on a baking sheet lined with waxed paper. Drizzle with olive oil and season with salt and pepper. Sprinkle the garlic over the tomatoes and bake for 20 minutes. Remove from the oven and increase the oven temperature to 400°F.

Set aside 8 sun-dried tomatoes and purée the remaining sun-dried tomatoes with a little of their preserving oil and the cumin in a blender or food processor, or rub through a strainer.

Arrange the reserved whole sun-dried tomatoes over the base of a baking pan and cover with the puréed sun-dried tomato mixture.

Finally, arrange the sliced baked tomatoes over the puréed sun-dried tomato mixture and top with the rolled-out pie crust dough. Bake for 25 minutes.

Serve garnished with the arugula leaves.

Tomato, basil and goats' cheese Tatin

Serves 6

2 x 14-oz cans peeled whole tomatoes

1 tablespoon olive oil

3 small white onions, chopped

bunch of basil, washed and chopped

3 small, round, dried goats' cheeses

2 eggs

¾ cup light cream

8 oz ready-made puff pastry

sea salt and freshly ground black pepper

arugula leaves, to garnish

Preheat the oven to 400°F.

Drain, seed, and chop the tomatoes, then fry in the olive oil with the onions and basil. Cook for about 15 minutes to make a thick sauce.

Remove the rind from the cheeses. Cut one cheese into small pieces and the remaining cheeses into slices. In a bowl, beat together the eggs, cream, and goats' cheese pieces. Season with salt and pepper and add the tomato sauce.

Arrange the goats' cheese slices over the lightly oiled base of a baking pan, cover with the tomato mixture and top with the rolled-out puff pastry. Bake for 25 minutes.

Serve garnished with the arugula leaves.

Grilled eggplant and pesto Tatin

Serves 6

2 lb eggplants

¼ pint olive oil

1 lb eggplant caviar
(see note)

1 jar (approx 5½ oz) pesto

1¼ cups pine nuts, toasted

8 oz ready-made puff
pastry

sea salt and freshly ground
black pepper

Preheat the broiler.

Cut the eggplants lengthwise into thick slices. Arrange them on the broiler rack, drizzle with olive oil and season with salt and pepper. Broil for 5–6 minutes on each side, brushing with olive oil as necessary and taking care that they do not burn.

Preheat the oven to 400°F.

Arrange the eggplant slices over the lightly oiled base of a baking pan, with the broader ends at the center to form a star shape. Spread with the eggplant caviar and the pesto, and scatter with the pine nuts, reserving about ¼ cup.
Top with the rolled-out puff pastry and bake for 25 minutes.

After turning out the Tatin onto a serving plate, scatter over the reserved pine nuts.

Note: Eggplant caviar is a specialty from the Provence region of France. It is available from some delicatessen stores and specialty shops.

Pear and Roquefort Tatin

Serves 6

3 firm green pears

8oz Roquefort cheese

3 eggs

4 tablespoons sour cream

8 oz sweet pie crust dough
(see page 5)

sea salt and freshly ground
black pepper

sliced red onion, to garnish

Preheat the oven to 225°F.

Peel and grate the pears.

Crumble the Roquefort cheese using a fork. Beat the eggs together with the sour cream, then add the Roquefort and grated pears. Season with salt and pepper, but go easy on the salt as Roquefort is already very salty.

Transfer the cheese and pear mixture to a baking pan and top with the rolled-out sweet pie crust dough.

Bake for 10 minutes, then increase heat to 350°F and bake for a further 20 minutes.

Serve garnished with the sliced red onions.

Spinach and feta cheese Tatin

Serves 6

1 lb spinach

2 oz butter

8 oz feta cheese

3 tablespoons milk

few pinches of French
4-spice powder (a blend
of white pepper, nutmeg,
ginger and cloves)

2 eggs, beaten

8 oz plain pie crust dough
(see page 5)

sea salt and freshly ground
black pepper

Pick over and wash the spinach, then fry in the butter in a skillet until the water it produces has evaporated completely. Drain the spinach again through a strainer, pressing down hard with a wooden spoon to remove all the liquid.

Preheat the oven to 350°F.

Crumble the feta cheese into a bowl, add the milk, season with pepper, and sprinkle over pinches of French-4 spice powder to taste. Add the eggs and stir well.

In a large mixing bowl, combine the spinach with the feta cheese mixture. Transfer to a baking pan and top with the rolled-out pie crust dough. Bake for 25 minutes.

Bell pepper and tapenade Tatin

Serves 6

2 red bell peppers

2 green bell peppers

2 yellow bell peppers

¾ cup mixed black and green olives, pitted

10 oz tapenade (olive and anchovy paste, available from delicatessen stores and some larger super-markets)

8 oz plain pie crust dough (see page 5)

sea salt and freshly ground black pepper

Preheat the oven to 350°F.

Wash the bell peppers, place them on a baking sheet lined with waxed paper, and bake for 20 minutes, turning regularly. When they are blackened all over, seal them in a plastic bag for 10 minutes. This will make them much easier to peel. Remove the skin and seeds, then leave the peppers to drain.

Increase the oven temperature to 400°F.

Cut the bell peppers into thin slices and crush the olives.

Combine the tapenade with the olives and season to taste.

Arrange the bell pepper slices evenly over the lightly oiled base of a baking pan, alternating the colors, then spread with the tapenade and olive mixture. Top with the rolled-out pie crust dough and bake for 25 minutes.

Bell pepper and garlic Tatin

Serves 6

1 bag broiled and skinned frozen bell peppers (see note)

1 cup olive oil

8 garlic cloves

8 oz ready-made puff pastry

sea salt and freshly ground black pepper

small bunch of fresh mixed herbs and cilantro, to garnish

Thaw the bell peppers according to the manufacturer's instructions on the packet and place them on a sheet of paper towels to drain.

In a large pan, gently heat the olive oil, add the garlic cloves, without removing the skins, and cook slowly for 15 minutes.

Preheat the oven to 400°F.

Drain and peel the garlic, reserving a little of the oil, then cut each clove in half.

Arrange the bell pepper pieces evenly over the base of a baking pan brushed with a little of the garlic cooking oil, season with salt and pepper and tuck the garlic cloves in among the bell peppers. Top with the rolled-out puff pastry and bake for 25 minutes.

Chop the fresh mixed herbs and the cilantro. Turn the tart out onto a serving dish and sprinkle with the chopped herbs.

Note: If frozen bell peppers are unavailable, prepare six peppers as for Bell pepper and tapenade Tatin on page 46.

Artichoke and anchovy Tatin

Serves 6

2 x 9 oz jars baby artichokes (or about 12) preserved in oil, drained

7 oz canned tuna in oil

20 anchovy fillets

1 jar Italian capers (about 3½ oz), drained

8 oz ready-made puff pastry

Remove the artichokes from the jars and drain on a wire rack or paper towels.

Preheat the oven to 400°F.

Blend the tuna with its oil, 5 of the anchovy fillets and the capers in a blender or food processor.

Arrange the 15 whole anchovy fillets in a star shape on the base of a baking pan, then place the whole artichokes between the anchovy spokes. Spread with the tuna, caper, and anchovy paste and top with the rolled-out puff pastry, taking care to seal the edges well. Bake for 25 minutes.

Onion and golden raisin Tatin

Serves 6

2 tablespoons olive oil

1 tablespoon argan oil
{available from delicatessen
stores}

2 lb frozen finely sliced
onions

1 clove

1 teaspoon grated fresh
root ginger (or ½ teaspoon
ground ginger)

1 heaped tablespoon
all-purpose flour

3 tablespoons sherry
vinegar

1 chicken stock cube

1¼ cups golden raisins

8 oz ready-made puff
pastry

sea salt and freshly ground
black pepper

Heat the olive and argan oils in a large skillet, then add the onions and clove and fry for 15 minutes until golden, stirring to make sure they do not stick. Add the ginger. Sprinkle over the flour, stir well, and then add the vinegar. Season with salt and pepper and cook for a further 10 minutes.

Preheat the oven to 400°F.

Dissolve the chicken stock cube in 2 cups boiling water. Soak the golden raisins in the stock for 20 minutes. Strain, discard the stock and mix the golden raisins into the onions.

Spread the onion and golden raisin mixture over the base of a baking pan. Top with the rolled-out puff pastry and bake for 25 minutes.

Delicious served with blue cheese.

Fig and pancetta Tatin

Serves 6

8 slices of pancetta

6 fresh figs

2 tablespoons olive oil

4 tablespoons balsamic vinegar

8 oz ready-made puff pastry

freshly ground black pepper

In a nonstick skillet, brown the pancetta slices on both sides, without adding any oil—it will produce enough fat of its own. Drain on paper towels.

Preheat the oven to 400°F.

Starting from the stalk end, cut the figs in half. Heat the oil in a skillet, brown the figs for 2 minutes on each side, then remove. Deglaze the pan with the balsamic vinegar, then reduce until the juices caramelize.

Pour the caramelized juices over the base of a baking pan, arrange the figs, cut sides down, evenly over the base, season with pepper, then cover with the pancetta slices. Top with the rolled-out puff pastry, taking care to seal it firmly to the sides of the baking pan, and bake for 25 minutes.

Zucchini and mint Tatin

Serves 6

2 lb small zucchini

2 tablespoons olive oil

bunch of mint

2 x 14-oz cans chopped tomatoes, boiled until reduced in quantity by half

3 eggs, beaten

8 oz ready-made puff pastry

sea salt and freshly ground black pepper

Trim the zucchini, cut them into quarters lengthwise, removing any seeds, then cut into 1$\frac{1}{4}$-inch chunks.

Heat the oil in a skillet and quickly fry the zucchini on all sides over a high heat until golden. Season with salt and pepper.

Preheat the oven to 400°F.

Chop the mint, reserving a few whole leaves. In a large mixing bowl, combine the tomato reduction with the eggs and chopped mint and adjust the seasoning.

Arrange the zucchini pieces evenly over the base of a baking pan, spread with the tomato and egg mixture and top with the rolled-out puff pastry. Bake for 25 minutes.

When cooked, remove the tart from the oven, turn it out onto a serving dish and garnish with the reserved whole mint leaves.

Belgian endive Tatin

Serves 6

2 lb Belgian endives

4 oz butter

few pinches of curry powder

2 tablespoons soft brown sugar

8 oz plain pie crust dough (see page 5)

sea salt and freshly ground black pepper

Trim the Belgian endives, then cut across in 1-inch pieces.

Melt 3 oz of the butter in a skillet and gently brown the endive pieces on all sides, turning frequently and carefully, then season with salt and pepper.

Preheat the oven to 350°F.

When the endive pieces begin to soften, after about 30 minutes, sprinkle with the curry powder and boil off any remaining cooking liquid.

Sprinkle the sugar over the base of a baking pan, dot with the remaining butter, then arrange the endive evenly, with the cut edges facing downward. Top with the rolled-out pie crust dough and bake for 25 minutes.

Broccoli and goats' cheese Tatin

Serves 6

3 heads of broccoli

2 scallions

bunch of chives

10 oz fresh goats' cheese

2 eggs

8 oz plain pie crust dough (see page 5)

sea salt and freshly ground black pepper

Cut the broccoli heads into florets, cook for 10 minutes in salted boiling water, then remove immediately with a slotted spoon.

Preheat the oven to 350°F.

Trim the scallions and chop together with the chives.

In a large mixing bowl, beat the goats' cheese and eggs together with the scallion and chive mixture. Season with salt and pepper.

Arrange the broccoli florets, stalk up, over the base of a baking pan. Cover with the cheese mixture, then top with the rolled-out pie crust dough. Bake for 25 minutes.

Mushroom Tatin

1 lb mixed exotic mushrooms (e.g. oyster, cep, chanterelle, chestnut, morel, etc.)

2 oz butter

sprig of thyme

1 tablespoon soy sauce

4 tablespoons sour cream

2 egg yolks

1 whole egg

pinch of grated nutmeg

pinch of curry powder

8 oz ready-made puff pastry

sea salt and freshly ground black pepper

Trim and wipe, but do not wash, the mushrooms. Chop the mushrooms into even-sized pieces, but not too finely.

Melt the butter in a large skillet, add the mushrooms and leaves from the thyme sprig. Fry gently until brown.

Preheat the oven to 400°F.

When the mushroom liquid has evaporated, add the soy sauce and stir well.

In a bowl, beat the sour cream with the egg yolks and whole egg. Add the nutmeg and curry powder. Season with salt and pepper and stir well.

Spread the mushrooms over the buttered base of a baking pan and cover with the sour cream batter. Top with the rolled-out puff pastry, tucking the edges in securely toward the base of the pan. Bake for 25 minutes.

Recipe texts: Catherine Quévremont
Copy-editor: Véronique Dussidour
Recipe production: Joss Herd and Susie Theodorou
Photographs: Deirdre Rooney

© Marabout 2003
This edition published in 2004 by Hachette Illustrated UK, Octopus Publishing Group Ltd.,
2–4 Heron Quays, London E14 4JP

English translation by JMS Books LLP (email: moseleystrachan@blueyonder.co.uk)
Translation © Octopus Publishing Group Ltd.

A CIP catalog for this book is available from the Library of Congress

ISBN: 1 84430 108 7

Printed by Tien Wah, Singapore